FRAUD

FRAUD

Donald Trump's Fake University
And Blueprint To Scam America

ART COHEN
with
DAN GOOD

Tampa, Florida

The content associated with this book is the sole work and responsibility of the author. Gatekeeper Press had no involvement in the generation of this content.

FRAUD: Donald Trump's Fake University And Blueprint To Scam America

Published by Gatekeeper Press
7853 Gunn Hwy., Suite 209
Tampa, FL 33626
www.GatekeeperPress.com

Copyright © 2024 Art Cohen

All rights reserved. No part of this book may be reproduced or transmitted in any form or by any means, electronic or mechanical, including photocopying, recording or by any information storage and retrieval system without written permission from the author.

The cover design is entirely the product of the author. Gatekeeper Press did not participate in and is not responsible for any aspect of the cover design.

Library of Congress Control Number: 2024944736

ISBN: 9781662955549
eISBN: 9781662955570

Dedicated to those who have fiercely fought for the precious freedoms that empower us to share our stories, experiences, and truths.

Contents

Introduction 1
Trump University Background 9
The Trump University Fraud 13
Updating the Record 29
Parallels 41
Wake-Up Call 61
Notes 65
Acknowledgments 69

Introduction

On a sunny afternoon in May 2024, a group of everyday Americans filtered into a drab New York City courtroom to announce their verdict against Donald Trump:

Guilty. Guilty.

Guilty.

For the first time in United States history, a former president was now a convicted felon—guilty on all thirty-four counts.

It was a verdict for America, and for all-time.

And yet, seven weeks later, following a favorable Supreme Court ruling, a delayed sentencing, and narrowly avoiding serious injury from a hail of gunfire at one of his rallies, Trump was standing on the Republican National

Convention stage in Milwaukee accepting the party's nomination and aiming for kingly coronation—his latest effort to stave off accountability. The frenzied stretch was capped off with Democratic President Joe Biden announcing that he wouldn't seek reelection and Kamala Harris, his vice president, becoming the Democratic nominee.

I've been hoping to see Trump held accountable for more than a decade—ever since I sued Trump in federal court in 2013 on behalf of other student-victims of his fraudulent education initiative, Trump University (I'm the Cohen in Cohen v. Trump) and helped to secure a $25 million settlement against him.

Long before Trump's political ambitions came into focus, I was duped by his promotion and puffery, and in 2009, I became one of the thousands of student-victims of Trump University who were drawn in by his lies of grandeur. His victims included veterans and retirees and single parents and dreamy entrepreneurs and me.

"Success, it will happen to you," he said in a pre-recorded video message played during our introductory seminar.

Trump University was a for-profit education initiative that promised to teach enrollees how to make money in real estate. Instead, the victims received none of Trump's insights and no education—the information provided was worthless and in some cases illegal.

The victims were everyday people. Many were seniors who lost their life savings. He dangled the dream of a better life in front of us, and all we got was debt and regret.

And all so he could make a quick buck, a motive that resonates to this very day.

Until recently, the Trump U settlement was the largest legal penalty of his career. But while my legal battle against Trump—along with other court challenges he's faced—were civil in nature, and thus came with financial and business ramifications, the trial against him in the spring of 2024 was criminal, and came with the potential for jail time.

Trump had been accused of falsifying business records in order to pay off people to keep them quiet—specifically the porn star Stormy Daniels—with the intent of illegally influencing the 2016 election.

Now, finally, Trump was getting a level of comeuppance.

Maybe that accountability could have come sooner if he hadn't carried out a different election interference campaign in 2016, one that resulted in his Trump University trials being pushed until after election day. I've pondered if the 2016 election could have turned out differently if he faced trial for Trump University and people could have learned the truth about his business "success."

All of these years later, we are still learning how unfit Trump was for office and the ways in which he illegally gamed the system to become an illegitimate president. The illegitimacy of Trump's presidency lies not in the lawful election process of 2016, but in his actions leading up to it. Trump conspired to privately threaten (and later publicly attack) a federal judge, resulting in the delay of his fraud trial until after the presidential election. This manipulation denied democracy a fair and open consideration of Trump's true nature and shady business practices.

Following his May 2024 conviction, Trump masqueraded as a victim once again, railing against the jurors, judge, prosecutor, his political opponents, and the legal system at large.

Trump, in failing to accept the results of the criminal trial that he lost—just as he failed to accept the results of a presidential election that he lost—and drawing in his sycophants and gutless followers on his attacks of the judiciary, is pulling the country deeper into authoritarianism and seeking to undermine and poison our institutions for his benefit.

Those efforts—and the danger Trump represents—became all the more clear on July 1 when his hand-picked Supreme Court ruled that he was immune from prosecution for some of the crimes he committed while in office.

Trump's tendencies are obvious, and he keeps using the same, tired playbook.[1] With Trump University, he could have made the whole thing go away for a penance, but didn't (sound familiar?). The legal proceedings dragged on through the 2016 election cycle (sound familiar?). Trump wanted to delay the proceedings, saying it was a politicized hit job

---

[1] As compared to the literal "Trump University Playbook" his team sought to hide, but that was revealed during discovery in the litigation.

meant to derail his campaign (sound familiar?), and after leveling attacks against the judge (sound familiar?), the trial was delayed until after the election.

After his 2016 election win, Trump—who vowed he would never settle—settled the cases (sound familiar?). Trump's organization then had to rely on the son of his convicted felon accountant (Allen Weisselberg) to free up the funds to make it all go away.

Eight years later, Trump faces additional legal challenges, ones he's fended off for the time being . . . and yet, the same elements are at play. It's a race between accountability and Election Day. And Trump historically has been really good at delay, delay, delay.

As we enter the 2024 election cycle, I couldn't stand idly by. I fear that the country I love—and the freedoms my father helped to defend during World War II in fighting against Nazi Germany—are slipping away. I wanted to do *something*. Anything.

Writing, again, seemed like the best outlet, just as it was three years ago when I published my first book, *Trump You: Promises, Lies, and Corruption: My Battle with Donald Trump's Fake University*, that I wrote with journalist and book writer Dan Good. That book contains full details of my yearslong legal battle and window into Trump's Dec. 10, 2015, deposition, including a hot-mic moment that spoke to Trump's ill intent.

Dan and I have teamed up again to write this supplement to *Trump You*. Important updates and insights have emerged since the publication of our book, and instead of releasing a new edition, we wanted to publish this addendum as a companion piece—a supplement to our earlier work as well as a standalone element.

We chose to name it *Fraud* because the word best encapsulates Trump's persona, his business career, and his time in office.

This supplement is organized into five sections:

- Background: A timeline of Trump University events

- The Trump University Fraud: A quick look back at the key details from the Trump University cases

- Updating the Record: New revelations about the Trump University saga

- Trump U Parallels: Considering the latest Trump legal and political updates through the lens of Trump University

- Wake-up Call: A look ahead to the 2024 presidential election

I'm encouraged by you reading these words—it means you're informing yourself about Trump's true nature. Read everything you can about him. Consider the body of work, the insults, and social media posts and slurry campaign statements and wonder if you can truly vote for him and still look at yourself in the mirror.

If I can change one vote in sharing my insights . . . that's part of my motive, sure, but this runs deeper. This effort is a means of continuing to put the facts and truth forward—and never to bow in the face of intimidation, threats, or evil.

Trump University Background

Key dates

2004: The Trump Organization files paperwork with the US Patent and Trademark Office for Trump University.

2005: Trump University launches as an online-only entity.

2007: Trump University begins offering live events.

2010: Amid waves of criticism and brewing legal action, Trump University changes its name to Trump Entrepreneur Initiative before shutting down.

Tarla Makaeff files a federal class-action lawsuit against Trump University covering anyone who purchased Trump University seminars from 2006 to the present, limited to the states of California, Florida, and New York. Trump University countersues, alleging defamation.

2013: Art Cohen files a lawsuit against Donald Trump in federal court seeking a national class action under the civil RICO Act covering all 50 states in the US.

New York Attorney General Eric Schneiderman sues Trump Entrepreneur Initiative LLC/Trump University, Donald Trump, and Michael Sexton in state Supreme Court in Manhattan seeking $40 million.

2014: The class is certified in the Makaeff case and Judge Curiel denies a motion to dismiss the Cohen case.

Art Cohen participates in a deposition hearing. A follow-up hearing is held the following year.

A nationwide class is certified in the Cohen case.

2015: Donald Trump announces he's running for president.

Trump sits for a deposition at Trump Tower on Dec. 10, 2015, during which time he's caught in a hot-mic moment discussing the case on a court video live feed.

2016: The start of the first federal Trump University trial is delayed from the summer until late November—after the presidential election.

Trump carries out his racist attacks against Judge Curiel and uses his platform on the campaign trail to criticize those trying to hold him accountable, including the lead plaintiffs.

Trump secures the Republican presidential nomination and months later, an Electoral College win to become the next president.

The sides hammer out a $25 million settlement deal to avoid going to trial.

2017: Trump is inaugurated as the 45th US President.

2018: The first distribution of settlement money is made.

2019: The final settlement money is distributed.

The Trump University Fraud

TRUMP UNIVERSITY—LIKE A lot of Donald Trump's ventures—was built on a lie.

The for-profit educational venture was founded in 2004 and launched the following year as an online-only entity featuring CD-ROMs, seminars, and consulting services. Even at that early stage, a New York state education official reached out to Trump's team warning them that Trump University couldn't use the term "university" and couldn't run live programs or other live training in the Empire State—it wasn't an actual, accredited university. But that warning was brushed aside, and it wasn't strongly enforced, and Trump University continued forward without changing its name.

After a few years, the online-only entity shifted to a live-course model. There was more money available in live courses held in hotel ballrooms. Dozens of such events were held across the country.

That was my entry to becoming a student-victim—I signed up for Trump University in 2009 after attending a live course event. I was excited at first. It took me a little while to realize I'd been had.

The Complaints Pile Up

Complaints against Trump University started emerging following each subsequent round of live events. Some of the students would get buyer's remorse after a few days or weeks, then come across the fine print—you only had three days to request a refund. Others would attend numerous seminars, looking to unlock value, before throwing in the towel.

One woman from Michigan claimed she and her husband spent $19,000 on a mentor program and "canceled immediately," but since they paid by check, they'd had trouble getting their money back.

"Does this sound like Donald Trump is an honest man concerned with helping you build wealth?" she wrote.

Another unhappy customer from California wrote that she "never would have paid if I had known that the info given to me was not true . . . I can't believe Donald Trump would allow such misbehaving to be associated with his name. Run fast and keep running where they are involved!"

Another commenter on a customer complaints website classified Trump University as "a well-designed scam using the name of Donald Trump who apparently doesn't care how much more Americans get hurt this year and the next ones by a weak economy. Instead, he's using it to take advantage of you."

Donald Trump had used his reputation as a real estate mogul and reality TV star to fleece thousands of Americans. But since the events didn't stay long in any one place, and since the experience played to its participants' hopes and fears, the situation's full scope took time to emerge. For those—like me—who struggled to get a return on their Trump University investment, we felt like *we* did something wrong, that our failure was a reflection of not trying hard enough, a reflection of our internal failings. We felt like we were the problem rather than the victim, which we were.

As wave after wave of complaints continued rolling in, the Better Business Bureau refused to accredit Trump University and gave it a D-minus rating.

Becoming Lead Plaintiff

Investigations and litigation picked up in 2010. A California resident, Tarla Makaeff, filed a class-action lawsuit against Trump University.

Early in 2011, an investigation from New York State Attorney General Eric Schneiderman's office kicked off, growing out of a broader look at for-profit education platforms. That year was also when I first joined the class of Trump University student-victims.

I didn't set out to become a lead plaintiff or personally

take on Donald Trump. It's a stressful, demanding role. I just wanted my money returned.

Makaeff's 2010 lawsuit, Makaeff v. Trump University, LLC, already had a lead plaintiff attached to it, along with named plaintiffs in Sonny Low, J.R. Everett, and John Brown. The attorneys chose those named plaintiffs strategically. Low lived in California, Everett in Florida, and Brown in New York. Makaeff's class-action suit covered residents in only those states—that's where the law firms located the bulk of the Trump University student-victims. A handful of other named plaintiffs in other states didn't have similar statutes to California, New York, and Florida regarding elder law and fraud and, therefore, could not join the class certification.

The lawyers tried to add to the Makaeff complaint, but Judge Gonzalo Curiel denied the motion. But there was nothing preventing a new complaint from being filed covering all states.

The attorneys also wanted to file the case under the RICO (Racketeer Influenced and Corrupt Organizations) Act—it's often reserved for mafia cases and other organized crime. It reflects offenses committed as part of an ongoing criminal organization.

Instead of suing Trump University again, the attorneys planned to file the new lawsuit directly against Donald Trump, given that Trump owned 93 percent of Trump University.

Like mobsters that create corporations to conduct their fraudulent activities, Trump's corporate shield was cracked, which left him vulnerable to personal liability. Trump's greed to own it all was his Achilles heel that opened him to a RICO.

After I joined the class, I had kept in close contact with the attorneys, and they thought my story resonated. So in 2013, they asked me if I'd agree to take on the lead plaintiff role for the national class-action RICO suit against Donald Trump, and after giving it some thought, I agreed.

Triple the Risk

Notably, since RICO judgments come with treble damages, if we won at trial, Trump would be on the hook for three times the actual damages, plus legal fees. So instead of the roughly $40 million that Trump University's student-victims paid, he could wind up being forced to pay more than $120 million himself. And that was a hefty total, even for a self-described billionaire like Trump.

Class in Session

I was deposed for the case in May 2014. Later that year, Judge Curiel decided whether to grant class certification, whether I was a suitable class representative, and whether my counsel was adequate to represent the rest of the class members and me.

If he rejected the motion for class certification, the class was effectively dead. And if myself or my counsel were not certified, it would significantly change our path forward—plaintiffs, including myself, would have to file separate complaints versus Trump. This may have resulted in thousands of cases throughout the country—costly for plaintiffs and Trump and a burden on the justice system.

Thankfully for me, and for other student-victims, we succeeded on all counts—Judge Curiel granted our class certification motion, appointed me as the class representative, and Robbins Geller Rudman & Dowd LLP and Zeldes Haeggquist & Eck as class counsel.

We were making progress on our cases.

And then, in June 2015, Trump rode down an escalator and announced he was running for president, which sent everything into hyper-drive and made the path to accountability that much more treacherous. And during this time from June 2015–November 2015, we tried to get a deposition date with Trump finalized. But numerous motions and excuses delayed the process. While we were trying to schedule Trump's day in court, he was doing everything he could—including "catch-and-kill" schemes involving the *National Enquirer*—to hold off negative press and get elected president.

Trump's Deposition and Hot-Mic Moment

Trump finally sat for a deposition in December 2015—but instead of simply answering questions like I had for my deposition, he grew furious and defensive, struggled to remember basic details, and acted like an oaf.

During a break in the action, Trump and his attorney, Daniel Petrocelli—with microphones still clipped to their jackets—continued talking as though no one was listening. I was watching the exchange as it happened on a court video feed. The moment revealed the types of coded directives and asks Trump makes privately and also exposed his ill intent.

"I've got hundreds of cases and I never get sued," he told Petrocelli.

Petrocelli tried explaining the situation in a way that would appease Trump. "Because they are saying you are personally involved in making false statements, and they can't prove that. That's the only reason," he said.

Trump remained inquisitive. I tried following the conversation but the audio was choppy due to cross talk and background noise.

"So, could you now, at the end of all depositions, go ask for the judge again, because I . . ."

"I'm going to have to think about it," Petrocelli said.

"Is he an asshole, or does he just want me in his courtroom?" Trump asked, emphatically pronouncing the insult in two syllables, ass-hole, as if he were mouthing it to someone across the room.

"The latter, I think," Petrocelli said.

"You really think so?" Trump asked Petrocelli about Judge Curiel. "You know him a little bit?"

"He's an average judge. He's on the wrong side of the aisle, too, that's not helping," Petrocelli said, a reference to Judge Curiel's being nominated by President Barack Obama.

Trump glanced around the room, as though he was making sure no one was nearby so they couldn't hear what he was about to say.

"What about the Spanish thing?" Trump asked. *The Spanish thing?!* Judge Curiel's parents grew up in Mexico, but Judge Curiel himself had been born in Indiana. Evidently, in Trump's mind, Judge Curiel was biased against him because of Trump's hardline anti-immigration and anti-Mexico stances.

"I got this guy, NOTHING," Trump said of Judge Curiel.

The conversation soon shifted to Judge Curiel's decision to certify the nationwide class, the centerpiece for the entire case.

"If we had it decertified, we'd essentially walk away," Trump said.

"Oh yeah, then it's over," Petrocelli responded.

"Didn't we almost have it decertified?"

"He had it half-decertified, exactly, because now everybody has to prove their own individual damages," the attorney said.

"Boom . . . maybe you get lucky."

At another point, Trump appeared to be giving his attorney a directive to tell Judge Curiel something. Something that could potentially cause Judge Curiel to decertify the class or throw out the case.

"Go in there and say that thing about him. Understand?" Trump asked.

"I'll give it a shot," Petrocelli said.

"You go ahead and give it a shot. Just do it."

"I'll see what I can do."

"And the other thing is . . . we'll wait."

"Let's wait. We'll talk separately."

"We give that a shot after this?" Trump asked. "You get a better shot after this . . . then boom . . . maybe you get lucky." As Trump said, "boom," he put his hands in the air, as though a mock explosion were going off, and for me, it might as well have been.

Setting a Trial Date

The campaign and Trump U cases trudged forward. Judge Curiel, in scheduling the Trump University cases for trial, had the authority to do what dozens of Donald Trump's Republican presidential challengers couldn't—take Trump off the campaign trail. If Judge Curiel scheduled the trial for August, which was the original plan, Trump would be forced to endure an embarrassing, painful fraud trial while running for president and required to tell the truth under the threat of perjury. And just eight years later, we are here today—with another fraud trial.

Wouldn't that be something?

And then came a May 6, 2016, hearing in San Diego. The hearing was a chance to discuss the time needed to try the case and the difficulties finding impartial jurors. There was always the concern from my counsel that jurors could find

Donald Trump not guilty simply because they supported him as a politician or if he turned on his charm on the witness stand. Or the reality that Trump could bring havoc upon jurors' lives, pushing private citizens performing their civic duty into the worst parts of the public sphere. If he had this little respect for a federal judge... where was his line? We've since learned that there is NO LINE that Trump wouldn't cross to intimidate others to help manipulate the legal system in his favor.

My counsel suggested a trial in late July or early August. Trump's attorneys wanted "to defer setting it for trial until after the nation's presidential election in November." A punt. A delay. The same argument Trump made for waiting to fill the vacancy left by the death of Supreme Court Justice Antonin Scalia. Let the voters make their choice, then things can be sorted out later. This once again has happened at the Supreme Court level—while debating absolute immunity for a president's actions while in office. Not his "official" duties, but actions a president takes that are personal and unofficial! And once again, the delay seems to have worked.

Petrocelli cited the "unprecedented circumstances" surrounding Trump's presidential run for the delay, and how the case had become a "lightning rod."

According to the attorney, Trump needed to devote his "full-time efforts and energies to running his campaign and running for office, and I don't believe that it would be fair to him—in fact, I think it would be a virtually impossible burden on him to have to defend himself at trial between now and

November." How farcical an argument that has proven to be in light of the recent trials that Trump is currently facing and still running a campaign for president.

Petrocelli suggested if Trump won the election in November, "we could pick a date after the election, sometime in the beginning of the year, and have our trial then. I don't believe there is any compelling reason, given that the case is already six years old, why it has to be tried now, particularly given the effects that it could have on the election process." Petrocelli's argument was very flawed because it was the election itself that should have mandated a trial as soon as possible. The American people have a right to know that a potential candidate for president is capable and above board. Politics is a transparent sport—needing a free press to expose the facts and positions of all candidates for the most important position in the world.

Judge Curiel asked whether the case could be tried between the election and inauguration.

"I would think it would be more reasonable to wait until after the inauguration because that is an extremely hectic time, when a president is putting together a transition team, making all sorts of extremely important appointments, not to mention you have a couple of holidays in there, with Thanksgiving and Christmas and New Year's," Petrocelli said. "And I would think, for example—early February is what I would propose be a reasonable time."

Ultimately, Judge Curiel was worried about the jurors and the court.

"I realize there's two aspects of holding a trial before the November election. One is in terms of Mr. Trump's availability to prepare, to participate in the trial. That's one thing. But then second is the—if not Pandora's box, the unleashing of forces that we can only speculate would occur in the event that we held a trial in this courthouse prior to the election date. We can look at the events of the last month or two to give us some indication of what might happen, and so to the extent that the past is prologue to what might happen, I am thinking of my jury. I am thinking of will they be able to stay clear of the media frenzy that will occur, that will arise? Will we be able to insulate them from events that may occur around this courthouse? So ultimately, that's my number one concern."

All of these years later, I'm skeptical that this truly was his number one concern. He made an argument to protect the jury; however, pushing forward till after the election would not have protected the jury any more than before the election.

I've always wondered if a sequestered jury would have been possible ... curiously, it wasn't discussed during the May 6 hearing. Was some backroom consensus reached? I have no personal knowledge of one, but it's interesting how everyone galvanized around this idea of a November trial start date. Judge Curiel's concern for the jury was genuine. However, I still wonder if his decision was primarily driven by concern for his personal and family well-being. What was that "thing about him" that Trump hinted to

Petrocelli would influence Curiel's stance on the trial? Was Curiel threatened in some way? Unless Curiel reveals his motivations, the true reasons behind his decision will remain a mystery. This uncertainty continues to haunt me and forced me to question the fairness and integrity of the entire process.

What the judge didn't know was that his decision to grant a delay represented a swing of a wrecking ball to the walls of democracy. The court, in acquiescing to Trump, deprived the American public of a crucial understanding of Trump's principles by permitting and advocating for a delay in Trump's trial until after the election. This denial of timely justice stripped voters of their right to fully assess the character and integrity of a presidential candidate, leaving the true nature of his actions obscured at a critical moment. By postponing the trial, they allowed Trump to avoid immediate scrutiny and accountability, manipulating the democratic process and undermining the transparency that is essential for informed voting. This act not only hindered justice but also betrayed the trust of the American people, similarly to how the delays in Trump's trial related to the Jan. 6, 2021, insurrection represented a serious loss for informed voting.

Attacking the Judiciary

Things were calm with the cases until May 27, when Judge Curiel ordered that the Trump University playbooks, the documents outlining instructors' tactics to generate sales, be unsealed and released.

"Defendant became the front-runner for the Republican nomination in the 2016 presidential race and has placed the integrity of these court proceedings at issue," Judge Curiel wrote in his opinion. *The Washington Post* had requested the documents be released. The judge didn't believe they contained anything of value or any proprietary information.

That date coincided with Donald Trump speaking in San Diego—and during that speech, he wound up discussing Trump University for twelve long minutes.

He proceeded to call Judge Curiel "a hater of Donald Trump, a hater. He's a hater." Trump read from a sheet and held his hand in the air. These remarks and attacks were prepared. "His name is . . . *Gon-zal-o Cur-i-alllll*," he said, dragging out the syllables, making the judge's name sound more ethnic while frumpling his chin and shaking his head and pausing amid the chorus of boos. ". . . and he is not doing the right thing."

In the days to come, Trump continued his attack on the judiciary.

"I have a judge in the Trump University civil case, Gonzalo Curiel (San Diego), who is very unfair. An Obama pick. Totally biased-hates Trump," Trump tweeted. He'd echo the line of attack against judges in future cases.

TV pundits continued asking Trump about his comments, and he only made things worse. He tried to argue to CNN's Jake Tapper that an earlier judge—who happened to be retired Judge Irma Gonzalez, also Mexican-American—was much fairer to him than Judge Curiel. "This judge is of Mexican heritage. I'm building a wall, OK? I'm going to do very well with the Hispanics, the Mexicans," Trump said.

"So no Mexican judge could ever be involved in a case that involves you?" Tapper asked.

"Well, he's a member of a society that's very pro-Mexico, and that's *fine* . . . it's all fine. But I think he should recuse himself." Ah, yes, Judge Curiel was a member of the Hispanic National Bar Association, which a year earlier put out a statement denouncing Trump's comments that Mexico was sending rapists and criminals into the country.

Tapper stood firm amid the bluster. "But you're invoking his race when talking about whether or not he can do his job," the TV journalist said.

"Jake . . . I'm building a wall, OK? I'm building a wall." *Trump's mouth hung open as he spoke, as though he was trying to breathe on Tapper.* "I'm trying to keep business out of Mexico."

"But he's an American."

"He's of Mexican heritage. And he's very proud of it."

Tapper tried to keep Trump on point.

"If you invoke his race as a reason why he can't do his job . . . ?"

"I think that's why he's doing it."

In a separate interview on CBS's *Face the Nation*, Trump was asked if he believed a Muslim judge might also be biased against him because he'd proposed a temporary ban on

Muslims entering the country. "It's possible, yes. Yeah. That would be possible, absolutely," he said.

A New Scam

With the Trump University cases delayed until after the 2016 election, Trump secured the presidency in early November, then, despite claiming he would "never settle," looked to make the whole thing go away. We wound up settling with him for $25 million.

The money was eventually paid out to the student-victims in two waves. But he had already moved on to a bigger scam—one aimed at deceiving all of America and threatening the very fabric of our nation.

Updating the Record

Jon Stewart was back in the anchor's chair at *The Daily Show*, the news satire show he'd departed nearly a decade earlier.

It was Feb. 13, 2024, his first night back. Stewart, older and grayer, but still just as sharp, planned to host the show once a week through the election. His voice was needed at this critical point because he has a way of getting to the actual truth in humorous, refreshing ways.

After some pleasantries, he got to the looming Trump-Biden presidential rematch.

"Nine months 'til the election, people!" he said. "And the exciting part is, we already know our candidates. It's . . . drumroll please . . . these fucking guys."

The segment centered around the candidates' ages and memory. A flimsy Special Counsel investigation had tried to paint Biden as forgetful when interviewed.

"This guy couldn't remember stuff during his deposition. Do you understand what that means?" Stewart said. "He had no ability to recall very basic things. Under questioning. The footage of the president unable to recall simple facts must have been brutal to watch."

And then a video played—of Donald Trump.

A video I had committed to memory.

The video I'd watched more than eight years earlier of Trump's deposition in my case.

The video I'd hoped would be seen widely as Trump previously ran for re-election in 2019.

The first clip showed Trump struggling to remember the names of any of the Trump University instructors.

A second clip showed Trump addressing his previous statements that he has one of the best memories in the world.

"I mean, I don't remember that, OK? As good as my memory is, I don't remember that. But I . . . I have a good memory."

"So you don't remember saying you have one of the best memories?" my attorney, Jason Forge, asked him on that fateful day in December of 2015.

"I don't remember."

Seeing Stewart, of all people, airing snippets of the deposition footage from Cohen v. Trump served as a reminder that this case still matters and that there are lessons we continue to learn about it. Some of those lessons have cropped up since the publication of *Trump You* in 2021. This chapter highlights new revelations and discoveries about the Trump University case that emerged in the past few years.

The Settlement Payment

Key *Trump You* passage: *On January 17, 2017, three days before he placed his hand on a Bible and swore to preserve, protect, and defend the Constitution of the United States as the 45th President of the United States, Donald Trump, and his Trump Entrepreneur Initiative made the $25 million Trump University settlement payment.*

Update: Amid the Trump University settlement being reached and approved in 2016 and early 2017, it wasn't fully clear to me, even as lead plaintiff, how Trump or his company secured the money for the settlement payment—the settlement agreement, however, mandated that Trump himself guaranteed its payment—not his Trump University shell company or any other shell entity. It's been long suspected that a deep-pocketed supporter of Trump's footed the bill. But I didn't know for sure, and that answer wasn't clear through the research and writing of the earlier book.

The facts: Making the payment, as it turned out, required the help of someone close to the Trump Organization—Jack Weisselberg, the son of longtime Trump Org. chief financial officer (and now convicted felon) Allen Weisselberg.

The younger Weisselberg worked as a "loan originator" at Ladder Capital. In 2017, the Trump Organization pursued a short-term loan to cover the $25 million Trump University settlement; it was revealed in court documents from the New York State civil fraud case against Trump and his company.

There was one problem: due to the Trump Org.'s lending covenants with Deutsche Bank, withdrawing the full amount would trigger a default. The favorable Ladder Capital loan helped Trump avoid a default.

I'd always wondered how perilous Trump's financial situation was and how a bigger payment could have crippled him or his company. It was interesting to learn how close to the edge he truly was, and in part, explained why he fought hard not to settle earlier despite the opportunity to remove the Trump University impending fraud case against him. He simply did not have the funds throughout 2016 to settle the case and only after winning the election in early November 2016 did he realize he must settle before taking the oath of office.

Tristan Snell

Key *Trump You* passage: *"The whole enterprise was not about building something bigger, or building a truly great company that was going to outlast him. It was about cash flow for him in the immediate present," Snell said.*

Update: Tristan Snell, the former assistant New York AG who guided the NY investigation into Trump University, and who was interviewed for *Trump You*, published a book of his own that I highly recommend, *Taking Down Trump: 12*

Rules for Prosecuting Donald Trump by Someone Who Did It Successfully.

The facts: There seems to be a lingering misunderstanding about the Trump University cases—and while the New York state case was important, the $4 million earmarked for New Yorkers represented only a fraction of the $25 million total settlement. New York State sued Trump and Trump University in August 2013, three years after Tarla Makaeff filed her class-action lawsuit and months before I filed my lawsuit.

Snell's media appearances have oversimplified and reduced everything. Yes, he played an important role in the NYS action, and the information he and his office gathered was beneficial to my federal case, but there were lots of contributors who helped to hold Trump to account for Trump University—it wasn't one person or one office, but a patchwork of people, and per Jason Forge's opinion to me that the RICO charges are primarily what drove Trump to find the money to settle the case.

Trump's "guy"

Key *Trump You* passage: *"Did you know we were rated D? My guy ... 'an Alan Garten type,' he's tough, gave them a call."*

Update: The audio from Trump's hot-mic conversation during his Dec. 10, 2015, deposition was choppy and difficult to follow at points, especially when he discussed the attorney who he claimed had confronted the Better Business Bureau to improve Trump University's rating. Upon further review, it now appears that Trump was referencing a longtime adviser, Boris Epshteyn, whose combative nature is well-known.

The facts: Epshteyn is an interesting figure in Trump's orbit—someone whose many connections, law degree, and brash, confrontational style have earned Trump's favor. He collaborated with Rudy Giuliani following the 2020 election and often attends court hearings with Trump, in addition to serving as a senior advisor for Trump's 2024 campaign. As the *New York Times* wrote in 2023, "As the former president faces escalating legal peril in the midst of another run for the White House, Mr. Epshteyn, people who deal with him say, mirrors in many ways Mr. Trump's defining traits: combative, obsessed with loyalty, transactional, entangled in investigations and eager to make money from his position."

Allen Weisselberg's time in the clink

Key *Trump You* passage: *I found it fitting that Weisselberg, who oversaw Trump University's finances and signed most of its checks, would find himself in handcuffs. And that the time frame over which this fraud occurred covered the entire life cycle of Trump University.*

Update: In 2022, one year after his arrest, Weisselberg pleaded guilty to fifteen criminal counts of tax fraud, including four counts of falsifying business records. And in 2024, he pleaded guilty again, this time to lying under oath while testifying in the New York AG's fraud case against Trump.

The facts: In revisiting Weisselberg's deposition testimony in my case from 2015, it's easy to poke further holes in his credibility.

"Throughout the time that you were overseeing these things at Trump University, as with all of the other of Mr. Trump's investments, you were acting on Mr. Trump's behalf, correct?" my attorney, Jason Forge, asked.

"Yes, of course," Weisselberg said.

"And you were ultimately . . . you're subject to his ultimate control, correct?"

"Yes."

During the deposition, he also discussed his salary and bonus structure, numbers that were later found to be enriched by untaxed perks. He also stated—erroneously—that he reduced his bonuses around the 2008 financial crash. "I wanted to set an example for my company," he said. "My kids are grown and I don't have the same needs I had many years ago. So I was fine with what I was making. I had no problem with it."

In actuality, he was receiving tax-free perks like a free apartment and private school tuition for his grandchildren.

As investigators uncovered, Weisselberg spent years

cooking Trump Organization's books—he falsified "hundreds of business records," investigators revealed. "Weisselberg understood that his assignment from Donald Trump was to have his reported assets increase every year irrespective of their actual values," authorities wrote.

If Weisselberg was subject to Trump's "ultimate control," as he said in 2015—and I have no reason to doubt that—I find it highly unlikely that his freewheeling ways were done in a vacuum without Trump's knowledge or direction.

Which is why, ahead of Trump's hush money trial in the spring of 2024, I emailed a section of Weisselberg's deposition transcript to the prosecution team handling the case. I needed them to see this crucial moment of honesty, this element of truth from a generally unscrupulous man.

I never got a response, and the exchange was never introduced as evidence during Trump's trial.

Instead, the prosecution relied on testimony from another of Trump's former henchmen, Michael Cohen, to further reveal Trump's micromanaging nature. As Michael Cohen told the court, Trump was closely involved with every aspect of the hush money schemes.

"Everything required Mr. Trump's sign-off," the fixer turned felon testified.

Trump University 2.0?

Key *Trump You* passage: *"We're gonna teach you about business; we're gonna teach you better than the business* *schools are going to teach you, and I went to the best business school. We're going to teach you better. It's going to be a shorter process; it's not going to involve years and years of your life. It's going to be less expensive, and I think it's going to be a better education. And it's going to be what you need to know. It's not going to be a lot of different theory that doesn't matter and will never be put to use. It's going to be what you need to know. So, we're going to teach you business, we're going to teach you life, we're gonna teach you salesmanship, and we're gonna teach you what you need to know. And we're gonna also make sure that no matter what you do, as I said before, you're going to love it. Because if you don't love it, it's never, ever going to work."*

Update: In a November 2023 post on his nascent social media platform, Truth Social, Trump announced his plans to launch an educational initiative called "The American Academy" to counteract, in his words, colleges "turning our students into Communists and terrorists and sympathizers of many, many different dimensions."

The facts: Where to even begin? During his rambling video announcement about "The American Academy," Trump claimed he planned to tax, fine, and sue large university endowments to fund the venture. "Its mission will be to make a truly world-class education available to every American, free of charge, and do it without adding a single dime to the federal debt," he said. Reading Trump's statements feel as if they are being pulled out of George Orwell's novel *1984*. Trump said that the academy would "gather an entire universe of the highest quality educational content covering the full spectrum of higher knowledge and skills," which sounds a little like a janky MasterClass. After saying that the initiative would be "strictly non-political," he made sure to draw the line and declare that "there will be no wokeness or jihadism allowed." Trump also suggested that the education level would be comparable to legacy institutions (sure) and that students would be able to complete their coursework "free and much more quickly." His promises that the offerings would be better, shorter, and less expensive all sounded too familiar. Thankfully, he learned one lesson by not calling it a "university" this time.

The bellwether

Key *Trump You* passage: *Trump and his ilk had claimed that Trump University was meant to help people achieve their dreams. But there was no deeper goal, no desire to give back, no benevolent aspirations for Trump to share his secrets. It was only about money.*

Update: Trump, along with his company and various company execs, were found civilly liable for engaging in rampant fraud in a series of rulings in late 2023 and early 2024 in New York, and Trump was on the hook for $454 million in penalties. The fraud case was brought by New York AG Letitia James after the Trump Organization for years overvalued assets to improve his, and the company's, financial position.

The facts: I found it notable that Judge Arthur Engoron, in issuing his decision about penalties for Trump and his organization, highlighted the company's "history of corporate malfeasance."

As he wrote, "This is not defendants' first rodeo."

He then summarized the Trump University legal battle and other Trump-related fraud cases.

"Accordingly, this Court finds that defendants are likely to continue their fraudulent ways unless the Court grants significant injunctive relief," he wrote. The financial burden imposed on Trump wasn't just because of some petty political clash or an arbitrary penalty, but a pattern of ongoing fraud. There is a direct line that connects Trump University with Trump's ongoing legal battles.

That line was highlighted during Michael Cohen's May 2024 testimony, when the witness highlighted his efforts to stiff Trump University vendors—and Trump's response.

Michael Cohen was tasked with renegotiating with Trump U vendors. Most settled for a fraction of the money they were owed. Two were never paid.

Michael Cohen recalled telling Trump about it to get credit.

"That's fantastic," Trump told him.

The admiration made Michael Cohen feel like he was "on top of the world."

Parallels

THERE ARE LOTS of parallels between Donald Trump's current and ongoing court cases and the Trump University legal saga—and exploring them reveals Trump's tendencies.

The things Trump says and does, while headline-generating and norm-breaking, are actually methodical and purposeful. They are meant to sow chaos, undermine the judiciary, foment his supporters' rage, and derail the cases against him.

I recognized that from studying him intently through my federal lawsuit against him, especially a hot-mic moment of his I witnessed from his Dec. 10, 2015, deposition.

Below, I've highlighted some of the key Trump University parallels with current circumstances involving the 45th president. The similarities are stark. His tactics have become more dangerous.

In a sense, the Trump University cases were a trial run, and the circumstances he's faced since leaving the White House reflect a refinement of his efforts.

The Endless Campaign

In 2023 and early 2024, as the many legal cases against Trump began to unfold, he and his attorneys cried foul that this was all an effort to keep him off the campaign trail. As he told a crowd in New Hampshire in August 2023, "How can my corrupt political opponent, crooked Joe Biden, put me on trial during an election campaign that I'm winning by a lot, but forcing me nevertheless to spend time and money away from the campaign trail in order to fight bogus, made-up accusations and charges?"

The first criminal case of his to reach trial, the hush money case in Manhattan that started in mid-April, largely kept him off the campaign trail. The case represented a two-fold problem for Trump: sidelining him while injecting the national discourse with lots of negative news *that he can't control.*

Trump University parallel: Trump's attorney during the Trump University cases, Daniel Petrocelli, lobbied on multiple occasions to delay the cases from reaching trial due to Trump's busy campaign schedule.

"It's unnecessary to set this trial before November. And I do believe that it will cause an unwarranted intrusion on the election process because this case will become a lightning rod in the political arena. It already has become that. It's been a recurring topic of discussion during the campaign so far. And beyond that, Mr. Trump must devote all of his full-time efforts and energies to running his campaign and running for office, and I don't believe that it would be fair to him—in fact, I think it would be a virtually impossible burden on him to have to defend himself at trial between now and November," Petrocelli said during a May 2016 hearing.

The delay tactic, of course, was successful, and the trial was delayed until November, after Trump's election win.

Failure to Turn Over Records

The government wanted its documents back.

After Trump left the White House, in January 2021, with boxes of documents that he wasn't supposed to keep—governmental records—the National Archives a few months later began asking Trump to return the records. Those requests continued, but Trump continued to refuse and ignored warnings, and the matter was passed to the Department of Justice.

Instead of handing over the records, Trump housed them at Mar-a-Lago. Sometimes, he was known to pull out documents and show them to people he was meeting with.

His attorneys provided some of the missing documents to the government, but Trump, authorities allege, continued to knowingly hold on to some of the stolen documents and had them moved around his property to avoid detection.

In August 2022, the FBI seized 102 classified documents. The Justice Department later stated that the situation calls

"Into serious question" statements by his legal team that they did their due diligence to find and hand over all of the documents.

Trump University parallel: The attorneys who represented Trump University's victims asked—repeatedly, and through discovery—about handing over any guidebooks that were given to instructors. For more than a year, Trump University's lawyers suggested such documents didn't exist.

But the documents did exist, in the form of a Playbook that outlined Trump U's guiding principles and practices. The playbooks documented every step of the marketing and recruitment process, from targeting potential student-victims to setting the venue's temperature (no more than 68 degrees). It also included tips for handling the media—"Reporters are rarely on your side and they are not sympathetic," a stance that wasn't all that far removed from Trump's eventual calls of "fake news" for unflattering coverage—and guidelines for actions to take if an attorney general arrived at a seminar location.

The Playbook unlocked the patterns behind the seminars. With the scripts in hand, you couldn't effectively argue that the problem was one or two rogue lecturers. The scripts showed that they were trained to spin stories about Trump and prey on people's vulnerabilities.

Attacking the (Unfavorable) Judicial System

If you are a judge or prosecutor who dares to stand up to Donald J. Trump, watch out.

Plan for everything about your life to get picked apart and criticized. You'll need extra security and a thick skin.

You'll receive death threats, too.

Trump has a way of unleashing all hell on any jurists, prosecutors, and court employees whom he considers unfavorable.

Ahead of his hush money/election interference trial in early 2024, Trump attacked Judge Juan Merchan and suggested that a social media post Trump (incorrectly) attributed to the judge's daughter made it impossible for him to get a fair trial.

"If the Biased and Conflicted Judge is allowed to stay on this Sham 'Case,' it will be another sad example of our Country becoming a Banana Republic," he wrote.

Justice Arthur F. Engoron, who presided over Trump's civil fraud case in New York, often faced Trump's ire—he was labeled "tyrannical and unhinged" and a "fully biased Trump Hater"—and he also received suspicious powder at his offices. Trump also blasted Justice Engoron's law clerk, causing the jurist to fine Trump and issue a gag order. Trump's attacks left the chambers "inundated with hundreds of harassing and threatening phone calls, voicemails, emails, letters and packages," the judge wrote in issuing a limited gag order.

Lewis A. Kaplan, the judge who oversaw his defamation

civil trial involving writer E. Jean Carroll—who Trump was found to have sexually assaulted decades earlier—was branded a "bully" and a "Clinton appointed, highly partisan, Trump Hating Judge."

Of US District Court Judge Tanya Chutkan, overseeing Trump's federal election interference case, he said that her "whole life is not liking me."

New York AG Letitia James—who secured a $460 million fraud decision against him in early 2024—was called "racist" and "a slob."

Fani Willis, the Fulton County, Georgia DA guiding the election interference case against Trump, was labeled "racist" by the former president because she happens to be Black, and he insinuated in 2023 that she "ended up having an affair with the head" of a gang she was investigating.

Special Counsel Jack Smith, prosecuting Trump's stolen documents and federal 2020 election cases, has been viciously attacked hundreds of times and labeled everything from a "Trump Hating THUG" to "deranged." Trump has also claimed that Smith's "wife and family despise me much more than he does."

One judge who hasn't faced his attacks? Aileen Cannon, the inexperienced Trump-appointed partisan hack handling his Florida criminal documents case, who keeps entertaining his attorneys' cockamamie delay tactics.

Trump University parallel: On May 27, 2016, the date that Judge Gonzalo Curiel ordered that the Trump University playbooks be released, Trump used a campaign speech in San Diego to trot out his attacks on the judiciary—calling Judge Curiel "a hater of Donald Trump" and highlighting the jurist's Mexican heritage, as though that had something to do with his rulings. The attacks, which Trump had plotted for nearly half a year at least, continued for weeks as a cover for the release of the embarrassing Trump U playbooks. The racist attacks were a cover for Trump. And when it was advantageous for him, he stopped insulting Judge Curiel and never mentioned him in public again.

Misogyny

Trump has a problem when women stand up to him.

Time and again, the thin-skinned brute has relied on misogyny to attack women. He treats women far worse than he does men in similar circumstances. He expects women to cave to his every wish—and when they don't, he can't handle women standing up to him.

As Sophie Gilbert wrote in the *Atlantic* for a feature that considered the ramifications of a second Trump term, "The misogyny that Trump embodies and champions is less about loathing than enforcement: underscoring his requirement that women look and behave a certain way, that we comply with his desires and submit to our required social function. The more than 25 women who have accused Trump of sexual assault or misconduct (which he has denied), and the countless more who have endured public vitriol and threats to their life after being targeted by him, have all been punished either for challenging him or for denying him what he fundamentally believed was his due."

E. Jean Carroll faced the worst of Trump's viciousness. After she came forward in 2019 to accuse him of raping her in a New York City department store in the mid-1990s, Trump denied the allegations, saying, among other things, that "she's not my type" and that they'd never met (they actually were photographed talking at a party years ago).

So Carroll sued him for defamation—once in 2019 and a second time in 2022.

He sat for a deposition in October 2022, at which time he mistakenly identified Carroll in a photo as his second wife, Marla Maples. He also hurled insults at Carroll's lawyer, Roberta Kaplan, accusing her of being a democratic operative and threatening to sue both Kaplan and Carroll.

A jury in 2023 found him liable in one of the cases for sexually abusing and defaming Carroll and ordered him to pay $5 million. Trump, unmoved, continued his attacks against his victim, blasting her in speeches and social media posts.

The second lawsuit went to trial in January 2024. As Carroll testified, "He shattered my reputation. I am here to get my reputation back and to stop him from telling lies about me."

A jury again sided in Carroll's favor—awarding her $83.3

million. The high cost was meant to deter Trump from making further statements about Carroll.

Even still, Trump wouldn't stop defaming Carroll. In a March 2024 interview on CNBC's "Squawk Box," Trump again claimed he'd "never met" Carroll, and that her sexual assault claims represented a "false accusation"—something the court already upheld as being believable.

Trump's difficulties being challenged by women were reinforced yet again with the announcement that Joe Biden was bowing out of the race for re-election and instead stepping aside for VP Kamala Harris to become the Democratic presidential nominee. Trump quickly attacked both her race and gender, calling her "weak" and "dumb as a rock" and saying that other world leaders are going to "walk all over her."

Trump University parallel: During a 2012 deposition, Trump targeted his interviewer, Rachel Jensen, telling her he would be suing her law firm "and you individually." She stood her ground and didn't give an inch. Trump didn't make the same claims in his second Trump U deposition to Jason Forge.

He saved his worst attacks against Tarla Makaeff, the first student-victim to file a Trump University lawsuit. Trump filed an anti-SLAPP lawsuit against her (a ruling in his favor was eventually overturned, and she was awarded $800,000). He insulted her on the campaign trail, and when, after six long years of battling Trump in court, she wished to withdraw as lead plaintiff, he attacked her some more, calling her a "terrible plaintiff."

Despite my suing Trump personally—where she had sued Trump University—Trump never attacked me publicly in the ways he did with Makaeff.

Delay, Delay, Delay

Judge Merchan was furious. Trump's attorneys wanted more time—a delay or a dismissal of his hush money case. In a March 2024 hearing, as the trial was set to begin, they suggested that they needed more time to review documents ahead of a trial date being finalized.

As his attorneys described it, there were "tens of thousands" of documents they needed to review (DA Alvin Bragg, meanwhile, estimated the figure at a few hundred of relevant documents).

Trump's team could have brought up their documents issues at earlier hearings—and requested documents they needed nearly a year earlier—but didn't. The jurist saw the late requests for what they were: obvious delay tactics.

"Why didn't you bring any of this to my attention? Why didn't you tell the court or anyone in the courtroom at that time that you had made this request, that it was taking a little longer than you expected?" Merchan asked. "So how come you didn't bring them up?"

If only other jurists—including a compromised Supreme Court—could call out and reject Trump's obvious delay tactics. The Trump-stacked Court entertained his frivolous claims that presidents deserve immunity from criminal prosecution for conduct during their tenure in office, that they are above the law.

The Court issued a stay on the issue in February 2024, scheduling oral arguments for late April—all but ensuring that Trump's federal election interference trial won't begin before the election.

As Mark Joseph Stern wrote for *Slate*, "On this timeline, the justices will probably issue a decision near the end of June. That punt gives Trump exactly what he wanted: an extended pause that will make it impossible for Judge Tanya Chutkan to hold a trial in time for the upcoming election."

Which is a complete travesty.

In his Georgia election interference case, a claim that prosecutor Fani Willis should be removed over her romantic relationship with a special prosecutor wasted weeks—and when she wasn't removed, the judge allowed for an appeal.

Another delay.

Trump's delay tactics have been entertained—and embraced—by the hack judge in his documents case, Aileen Cannon.

As Dennis Aftergut and Laurence Tribe wrote in early 2024, "Our legal system entrusts trial judges with a wide swath of discretionary decisions in ruling on evidence, framing jury instructions, and controlling other facets of the cases they try, with barely any appellate supervision. As a result, it's difficult to imagine that anything approaching justice will emerge from a criminal proceeding over which Cannon presides in which the fate of her benefactor, and thus her own career, is at stake."

Trump University parallel: Judge Curiel could have brought one or both of the Trump University cases to trial in 2016, but in May of that year, as the presidential race was coming into focus, he decided to delay the trials until after the election—a critical delay that had massive implications for our country. At the time of the delay, Judge Curiel cited "the unleashing of forces that we can only speculate would occur in the event that we held a trial in this courthouse prior to the election date."

But wouldn't those "forces" have been present whenever a trial was held?

And couldn't Judge Curiel have taken steps to protect his jurors, such as using an anonymous jury where the jurors' names were withheld?

By caving to the pressures unleashed by Trump, Judge Curiel helped to ensure that details of Trump's conning everyday Americans—and the fiction of his business success—wouldn't come out during the election cycle.

RICO

RICO (Racketeer Influenced and Corrupt Organizations Act) is a statute typically applied for organized crime syndicates—and Trump's criminal operation certainly applies.

It means a pattern of crimes were used to support a corrupt enterprise.

Which is why Fulton County (Georgia) DA Fani Willis slapped Trump and his cronies with a RICO charge in the Georgia election interference case.

Trump University parallel: One of my attorneys, Jason Forge, pushed to include RICO in my 2013 civil lawsuit against Trump. That possibility became an option after we learned that Trump owned 93 percent of Trump University—the organization was effectively him, and the corporate shield was cracked.

Notably, a guilty verdict in a federal RICO lawsuit comes with triple, or treble, damages, meaning he could have been on the hook for a massive amount of money if a jury ruled in my favor.

Refining His Ability to Take Americans' Money

Donald Trump needed money bad. Again.

So he made appeals to small donors, claiming he "could be locked up for life" and that he needed donations to keep his campaign moving forward during his New York criminal trial in the spring of 2024.

Small donors—everyday people—have helped to prop up Trump for years. And he continues to prey on their fears, seeking their money while indifferent about their situations and suffering.

Trump University parallel: Trump U was a less refined way for Trump to separate people from their money. In Trump University, Trump was selling hot air with the promise of a high-quality education—and it would come back to bite him, to the tune of the $25 million settlement. As a candidate, Trump can sell the American public hot air and not have to face the threat of a lawsuit for not fulfilling on his promises.

Election Interference

Trump's 2024 hush money/election interference case in New York laid bare the efforts he was taking to keep negative coverage out of the public discourse during the 2016 election cycle.

The efforts at the center of the trial involved his collaboration with *National Enquirer* publisher David Pecker to both plant negative stories about his rivals—in this case, Ted Cruz—and to keep quiet any stories about sexual encounters involving two women, Karen McDougal and Stephanie Clifford, the adult film star known as Stormy Daniels, in "catch-and-kill" schemes.

Trump University parallel: Notably, the negative stories against Cruz were published as Cruz was drawing blood in his attacks against Trump, hammering him about, among other things, Trump University and Trump's record as a husband and philanderer.

Attempting to keep negative stories about yourself from

being published in itself isn't a crime; the crime, as prosecutors have laid out, involves falsifying business records with the effort of influencing an election.

As the case unfolded, it made me wonder if Trump's efforts in Trump U—like raining down hell on a federal judge to delay the cases against him—could similarly amount to election interference.

Trump the Decision-Maker

Trump has long sought to distance himself from criminality by claiming that he wasn't the person taking actions or making decisions.

But that argument falls flat on its face when considering that the Trump Organization has long operated as a mom-and-pop business with very few decision-makers and major decisions needing Trump's approval.

During his election interference trial in New York in early 2024, Trump's former White House communications director Hope Hicks spoke of Trump's hands-on approach with messaging during the 2016 campaign.

"We were all just following his lead," she said.

Trump University parallel: The idea of Trump as a micromanager and decision-maker was also noted by Allen Weisselberg during his 2015 deposition in my case.

"Throughout the time that you were overseeing these things at Trump University, as with all of the other of

Mr. Trump's investments, you were acting on Mr. Trump's behalf, correct?" my attorney, Jason Forge, asked.

"Yes, of course," Weisselberg said.

"And you were ultimately . . . you're subject to his ultimate control, correct?"

"Yes."

Trump has long claimed that bad actors—such as Weisselberg and Michael Cohen—were acting on their own when they took poor or illegal actions. But that suggestion has been refuted at many turns.

"Stealth" Juror

As the prosecution in Trump's election interference/hush money case rested their case in May 2024, and the trial reached closing arguments and was handed to the jury for deliberations, concerns arose over a "stealth" juror—one who was always going to decide in Trump's defense, no matter what. Just one pro-Trump juror could cause the case to end in a hung jury.

Trump University parallel: Trump had a telling exchange during his Dec. 10, 2015, deposition.

"You mean if I get one juror, I win the trial?" he asked his attorney, Daniel Petrocelli.

Petrocelli corrected him: "They don't win."

"Meaning they don't win," Trump said. "Wow, I like that. I like those odds."

"So do I," Petrocelli said.

You could see Trump's mind in motion as he spoke on the topic—he liked his chances, and his ability to manipulate people to do his bidding.

Keith Schiller

Trump's longtime bodyguard was connected to two important moments recounted during the 2024 hush money election interference trial.

The first was Trump's 2006 Lake Tahoe encounter with Stormy Daniels; Schiller had been in touch with Daniels and urged her to visit with Trump.

In October 2016, just ahead of the presidential election, Schiller was nearby Trump again—and Schiller passed the phone to the boss so Trump could hear that the deal to keep Daniels quiet had been finalized—according to Trump's former fixer, Michael Cohen.

Trump University parallel: During a break in Trump's 2015 deposition, which I watched on a live video feed, Trump received updates from Schiller about calls he had received, in that case, from the then chief executive officer of the PGA of America Pete Bevacqua. Schiller was in Trump's inner circle, and seeing their exchanges about messages and phone calls aligns with Daniels' and Michael Cohen's testimony that Schiller played a key role in their contact with Trump.

Coded Language

Trump often speaks in coded language, especially when discussing directives and nefarious plans carried out by his lawyers and consiglieres. For Michael Cohen and his reimbursement for paying for Stormy Daniels' silence, Trump referred to it in a phone conversation as "that other thing." For Ukraine ambassador Marie Yovanovitch, forced out through a pressure campaign by Trump and Rudy Giuliani to damage Joe Biden's reputation, Trump suggested to Ukraine's president that Yovanovitch would "go through some things." Trump's coded language parallels the talk of mob bosses and leaders of organized crime—and picking up his speech patterns and veiled language suggests preconceived plots and nefarious intent.

Trump University parallel: During Trump's hot-mic conversation on Dec. 10, 2015, he lowered his voice and whispered as he urged his attorney to confront Judge Curiel about "that thing about him," and also noted "the Spanish thing," Judge Curiel's Mexican-American heritage. Whether Trump was referring to Judge Curiel's heritage when referencing "that thing about him," or something else involving himself or his family, isn't entirely clear, but it speaks to Trump's intent and parallels other coded language he used at critical moments.

Attacking a Judge's Heritage

As the prosecution rested its case in May 2024, Trump stood outside of court, railing against the Colombia-born judge overseeing his hush money trial. "The judge hates Donald Trump. Take a look. Take a look at him. Take a look at where he comes from," Trump said of Judge Juan Merchan. "He can't stand Donald Trump. He's doing everything in his power." Notably, Judge Aileen Cannon, the toady jurist undermining and delaying his classified documents case, was also born in Colombia—but for some reason, Judge Cannon's background hasn't become a focus for Trump.

He leveled attacks against the Democratic presidential nominee for her mixed-race heritage, too. Speaking at a National Association of Black Journalists convention in July 2024, he repugnantly suggested Harris was Indian-American but "became Black" for political gain. "Is she Indian or is she Black?" he asked.

Trump University parallel: In 2016, Trump went on the attack against the Indiana-born Judge Curiel, calling him a "hater" and suggesting his Mexican-American heritage was the reason why (an earlier judge who had ruled in his favor with Trump U, Judge Irma Gonzalez, also Mexican-American, had been spared his racist attacks). The vitriol against Judge Curiel continued for weeks. It was a chance for Trump to undermine the judiciary, galvanize his base, and knock other negative stories out of the news cycle.

Wake-Up Call

After Kamala Harris became the presumptive Democratic presidential nominee just months ahead of the 2024 presidential election, an image of a check was shared across social media.

The check, dated from September of 2011, was for $5,000, made out to "RE-ELECT ATTORNEY GENERAL KAMALA D HARRIS 2014" and signed in Trump's thick sharpie scribble signature.

Trump, as it turned out, wanted to make sure states didn't investigate Trump University, so he attended a fundraiser hosted by then New York Attorney General Eric Schneiderman and pledged his money to the woman who would run against him for president more than a decade later.

In the end, it all comes back to Trump University.

Donald Trump is still a grifter, fraudster, scam artist, cheater, huckster, draft dodger, media manipulator, and snake oil salesman, and now, a convicted felon. And as such, he lacks character for any position of power over others and certainly not for the presidency.

He has spent his entire public life—and especially his political career—pouring gasoline on the institutions upholding our democracy, and every vote for him is a lit match.

Trump doesn't care about making the country great, or better, he only cares about making it great or better *for him*. He only cares about greed and self-enrichment. His disrespect for those who gave their lives for our country shows his lack of patriotism—he cares little for those who sacrificed their life for the liberties gotten from our Constitution, written almost 250 years ago.

He has radicalized the Supreme Court and judiciary with his far-right appointments, turned the GOP into a cult of personality, fueled chaos and polarization on Capitol Hill, and weakened the United States' international standing. He is a shill who—in desperate need of cash—is compromised to the highest bidder.

If reelected, he seeks to weaponize the military and government so he can enact revenge. He vows to adopt draconian, evil detention and deportation measures against immigrants and take away women's body autonomy. He could effectively dismantle and reorganize our government to fit his needs. He will undermine our international alliances, cozy up to strongmen, and disrupt peace and order on the global level.

His extreme isolationism, racism, and anti-immigration positions will all make America weaker. His economic policies and agenda would worsen, not improve, inflation.

His transactional actions without regard for the law will fracture an already compromised legal system.

His orders and acts will effectively give him kingship—borrowing other modern authoritarian tactics.

He isn't the first American to have kingly or authoritarian ambitions. In Rachel Maddow's podcasts and Monday-evening program on MSNBC early in the 2024 election cycle, she spoke to the many failed attempts of third-party candidates' aspiring kingship. However, the names are lost in history because they ran on third party platforms because neither major party would accept their principles. Even Trump's first attempt in 2000 as a third-party candidate under the Reform Party has faded quickly from most people's memories because of the lack of serious recognition.

But he isn't simply some braggadocious celebrity making a failed political bid. Trump represents a clear and present danger.

After Trump deceived me, it took me a long time to get past my personal embarrassment. How had I been so stupid? How had I believed his lies?

I know everything is so politicized today, but before voting for Trump in November, you should remember that he isn't going to make your life better, he's inevitably going to make things worse.

Think back to his mismanagement of the country's response to the COVID-19 pandemic, a response that cost hundreds of thousands of additional lives (and let's not forget his suggesting light and bleach as COVID treatments).

He lost bigly on trade deals with China, requiring the US government to bail out farmers for tens of billions of dollars. And after he lost the 2020 election, he fomented a mob to attack the US Capitol and declined to adhere to the peaceful transfer of power.

You could be in 100 percent support on his policies and simply see his presidency as a means to an end—but he will burn you too, eventually, just like he burned me.

It's time to turn Trump away once more.

You can make sure he's removed from public life—now and forever—or come to regret your support of Trump because you realize too late you've been scammed.

Trump is now trying to scam America once again. Embarrassment about my participation in Trump University will remain indefinitely.

If you want to learn more about what Trump embarrassment feels like, or my court battle against Trump, visit https://www.artcohenauthor.com/ or reach out to me artc@artcohenauthor.com.

Trump University, in essence, was Trump's trial run of stealing from the American public and selling them hot air—an effort he's since honed and refined.

This fall, American voters are his targets. Our democracy hangs in the balance. If you place your faith and support in Trump, the consequences will inevitably follow. The stakes are too high to ignore; our future depends on making the right choice.

Notes

This book relies on the author's personal notes and recollections, eight years of court filings, and media coverage.

Documents from the two federal Trump University lawsuits—3:10-cv-00940-GPC-WVG Low v. Trump University, LLC et al (the Makaeff/Low case) and 3:13-cv-02519-GPC-WVG Cohen v. Trump (the Cohen case)—can be found on PACER (Public Access to Court Electronic Records) at https://pcl.uscourts.gov/.

The information reported in this book pulls from a wide range of sources, documents, and news reporting, and we've noted those that provided significant contributions below.

Background

The chapter relies heavily on the author's personal recollections and the details from his lawsuit, 3:13-cv-02519-GPC-WVG Cohen v. Trump. To view the Trump University promotional video, visit https://www.youtube.com/watch?v=4q1N_B6Y4ZQ.

To view video clips from Donald Trump's Dec. 10, 2015,

deposition, and to read about the context of his statements, visit "Donald Trump Wanted to Keep This Video Deposition Secret. We Got a Copy" by David Corn and *Mother Jones* published on Sept. 18, 2020 at https://www.motherjones.com/politics/2020/09/donald-trump-university-fraud-lawsuit-deposition-full-video/. You can also view video of Trump's hot-mic conversation at https://www.motherjones.com/politics/2020/08/new-hot-mic-video-what-trump-told-his-lawyer-when-he-didnt-know-a-camera-was-rolling/. Trump's deposition transcripts were filed in court in June 2016 and are available on PACER.

Updating the Record

Jon Stewart's discussion about Donald Trump's 2015 deposition video on *The Daily Show* is available online: https://www.youtube.com/watch?v=NpBPm0b9deQ&t=295s.

Details about the efforts to make the payment in the Trump University settlement, including Allen Weisselberg's son and the short-term loan through Ladder Capital, was included in a February 2024 court filing connected to the New York fraud case against Trump and the Trump Organization. It's available online:

https://iapps.courts.state.ny.us/fbem/DocumentDisplayServlet?documentId=CJKA2EOIiTRatUAYz6FyeA==&system=prod.

Parallels

Sophie Gilbert's sobering read from the January/February 2024 issue of The *Atlantic*, "Four More Years of Unchecked Misogyny," is available online:

https://www.theatlantic.com/magazine/archive/2024/01/trump-sexual-abuse-misogyny-women/676124/.

Acknowledgments

Art Cohen

I extend my heartfelt gratitude to all those acknowledged in my previous book *Trump You*. Without your support, this supplement would not have been possible. Special recognition goes to Zimin Cohen for the exceptional cover design of this book. I also want to express my deepest appreciation to my wife, Jackie, who has been my unwavering bedrock of support. Finally, I would like to thank Dan Good, my writing partner, whose professionalism and dedication helped me complete this work in record time.

Dan Good

To Suzy and Dean, whose love and support mean everything to me. I'm inspired by those who stand up for what is right. Art, it's been an honor and privilege to work together again and bring this important message forward.

www.ingramcontent.com/pod-product-compliance
Lightning Source LLC
LaVergne TN
LVHW011739060526
838200LV00051B/3243